Pick of the crop

The poetry collection

Bob Woodroofe

Greenwood Press

First published in Hardback 2017

This edition in Paperback 2019

Greenwood Press
38 Birch Avenue
Evesham
Worcs. WR11 1YJ

Tel 01386 446477

http://www.greenwoodpress.co.uk

Many of these poems have previously been published in various poetry magazines and performed at readings

Photographs Bob Woodroofe

Copyright © 2017 & 2019 Bob Woodroofe

Bob Woodroofe has asserted his right under the Copyright, Design & Patents Act 1988 to be identified as the author of this work

A CIP catalogue record is available for this book in the British Library

ISBN 978-0-9952790-2-5

Dedication

This collection is dedicated to

my daughters

*Emma, the dark and quiet one,
without whose instigation I would
never have followed this path.*

*Sally, the blonde and bright one,
taken from us far too early, who sadly,
didn't get to read some of these.*

*My Grandchildren and Great Grandchildren,
amongst whom, I hope, there is one
to carry this torch onwards.*

*and finally to Sue Johnson
without whose constant inspiration,
support and love, this collection
would never have seen the light of day.*

Contents

Rural and Countryside	*1*
Nature	*9*
Famous poems	*19*
Worcester and Cathedral	*27*
Evesham and the Vale	*37*
Croome	*47*
Inspirations	*55*

Rural and Countryside

Inspiration from living on the edge of and working in the Countryside

Cutting comment   2
Five furrow reversible   3
Extraction   4
Inland sea   5
Smallest under roof ridge   6
Hand in hand   7
Hard row   8

Cutting comment

set the angle fade work the whetted blade
draw across the stone hone to feather edge

the snaith's moulded curve folded to body
the nib on the shaft slipped under the rib

the ease of stance moves with a sideways glance
body's inclined weight feet toeing the line

watch the arms long bend extend to full length
limb and tool duet beads sweat on the brow

the age old rhythm with so light a touch
measures the distance closes to the ground

with each even stride forward swing and glide
deep into the swathe in the cut grass bathe

song of steel through air sounds against the stem
soft tumble of grass time and time again

the keen of the blade spares nothing at all
sharp enough to slice the words from the page

Five furrow reversible

a single furrow drawn through
dark soil across stubbled field
hugs the curve of land
one follows another a boy
and the single power of horse

shares slice brown earth
bite into ground behind green John Deere
how many horses power to turn furrows
as the throb of revolutions rise
and five plumes spurt over steel

gulls froth at the cut faces
pounce on worm and grub
turned to the light their stark white
peppered with black of rook
as furrow fingers spread across the field

time and again to the headland
tractor harnessed to the furrow
hands on controls power at their bidding
the polished blades flash in the sun
as they turn then thud into place

cut deep down into the land
five furrows straight as a die
hand over hand span the field
air conditioned cab radio on
oblivious to the spectacle

Extraction

crescent swifts sweep the sky
wheel in ceaseless circles
screaming overhead

here by the pools
the white flash of martin's breast
startles over the bank

sand gravel pebble
sifted and graded
piled into rows

bullet of belemnite
the poke of devil's toe nail
whorl of ammonite

from the dead to the living
out on the sea of fields
lit by a low evening sun

the catcher rescues a swan
folds into a carpenters bag
to the jangling of corn buntings

Inland sea

no pull of tides
nor foam flecked tops
as wind blown waves
break on the eye

no beach to pound upon
yet surf sounds in the ear
no swimmers in the shallows
nor life upon the shore

no wake or wash from yachts
that hug the headlands
line astern before the wind
anchor down the edges

no boat astride the horizon
no tang of salty air nor
breath of ozone rides the breeze
floats over green-housed ground

Smallest under roof ridge, largest over eaves

From Michaelmas to December chase thin tile
through shafts and tunnels as intimate as wives.
Mine slivers of flaggy stone, hewn honey brown,
bedded in the slaty darkness of Stonesfield pit.

Stack the 'pendle', wait till the cold of January
fingers the edges. The ring of church bell rouses,
by moon's light shadowy figures attack the clamps,
strew slabs on stiffening grass for icy hands to cleave.

Frost split, hear the tap of Summer pick and hammer,
squat in hazel hurdle pen mounded round by spoil.
Shape and pierce thin sheets, cut coral, urchin, shell.
Rain from ancient seas raised to sheltering roof.

No frost then no work, simply left to bury deep,
keep water in or they'll be bound and never split.
Now in the quarry quiet only moss fingers stone,
the last tile makers have long left their second home.

Hand in hand

A landscape created by hands, worn by time and labour,
they have caressed this moorland to a garden of plenty.
Turned thin acid peat to warm rich soil.

Small beds surge with life. Hand sown seeds drink cold rain,
reach for light, break through into skylark soaked blue.
Trees burst with blossom in cool high air.

The garden in return has shaped the hand,
honed and fed the body and mind that created it.
The hands are large and rough,
but full of a gentle tenderness.

Hands that lovingly cup the violet beetle,
the fluttering moth. Fingers on which ladybirds perch,
launch red shelled into the breeze.

Nails abraded against stone,
eroded by constant passage through soil.
See the scars from rock and knife marked on skin.

Each line on the worn palm reflects one of its features,
here a flower bed, a path, steps leading to a rockery,
a seat by the pond for rest.

The parts of the garden reach like fingers
into the whole of the land.
Garden and hand intertwined.
Growing together.

Hard row

scratch dirt break the tilth slice concrete ground
blade chops puffs of dust every jab and draw
short tread once again shuffle the row
slash down hoe between sprouts growing green

fray hand jar the arm earth much too dry
mouth parched rasps warm air longs for cold tea
slake thirst wet the lips bottled in hedge

gnaw crust chew hard cheese rest in cool shade
rub stone keen the blade sharpen the edge
slow steps trudge the row grind hedge to hedge

rays burn cap shades focused on crop
beats neck sweat ruts dust mahogany grain
thin out whittle down crawl across field

earth cakes trousers boots encrusted film
each row hack again acre after acre
flay soil flog the body till the final ache

Nature

Fascination with and passion for nature in all its shapes and forms

Eel	*10*
Hipton	*11*
Lucky or not	*12*
New clothes	*13*
Riders of the film	*14*
The tiniest of birds	*15*
Urchin	*16*
Birds in scarlet berries	*17*
Terrorists	*18*

Eel

fish with no scales mucus slippery
writhe silver in storm moons light
glide through wet grass breathe through skin
exist on stores of fat unable to feed
from pond and stream answer the craving
drawn down by the tidal urge
hungry for salt and sex
plunge to the sea and west
over the shelf to depths of darkness
lengthened by the shift of continents
a journey to die for no return

life prevails from wasted bodies
spawned deep in the sea of weeds
they rise up drift on currents
feed and grow reach the coast
slivers of glass through channel tides
shoaling Severn Sharpness Frampton
Newnham beyond slip nets climb weirs
Wainloads Tirley Apperley on
to where ancestors lived and dreamed
Tewkesbury Bredon Evesham home
each imprinted in their genes

Hipton

Out in the quietness of evening fields
long tufts of grass pull at our legs
as we wade through them
towards the overgrown hedge.
Towards the brambles that snake
around our shins, trip us up,
scratch our outstretched arms.

We filled punnet after punnet,
that bubbled over with the black fruit.
Purple fingered we watched
spellbound as the huge orange ball
dropped towards the hill.

Dark clouds suddenly settled over us,
moved first one way, then the other.
Blotted out the setting sun, the whirr
of thousands of wings ever louder.

Trees grew more and more leaves,
whistles and calls grew in volume,
till dumbstruck we staggered
back across the fields and out
of the deafening murmuration.

Watched and listened till all
was quiet and still and as
the sun finally sank beyond the hill,
we carried our black bounty home.

Lucky or not

fed well on trefoil and vetch
the poison molecules stored
winter lost amongst the grass
then climb their thin ropes
spin silk to parchment
swell the narrowness of stems
the shucked black skin
crumbles between fingers
ash spread on the wind
in the light of day not night
whirring warning into flight
crowd and jostle to feed
on blue scabious purple knapweed
magenta spots on deepest black
red for danger six for luck

New clothes

open wide the iris of your eye
when you go down to the woods today
through the aperture have vision to view
he who fed from the spreading sallow

yet now he rises to the tallest oaks
hunts a mate through leafy green
see him fight flash bright in sun
then quench his fire from puddles

drawn down to the rottenness of life
now dressed in resplendent brilliance
the purple sheen unparalleled
lights his grand imperial majesty

Riders of the film

Molecular force holds the meniscus,
pulls it into the liquid body, as you
skate over the tensioned skin.

Pads of hair dent the surface,
repel and push the fluid down,
never sink in, never get wet.

Four indentations cast shadows
that float over the sunlit bottom
as you scull over the film.

Sense the vibrations, ripples
that spread from prey that drowns,
stride over to suck it dry.

Fly to winter shelter,
in spring return,
walk once more on water.

The tiniest of birds

came to my window
picking at insects
on the cotoneaster branch
a short distance from the glass

so intent on his reflection
he seemed oblivious of my presence
as I approached from the other side
only inches between us now

the constant flick flick of wings
his agitation obvious
the livid crest of gold raised
displaying his aggression

suddenly the light was cut
by the brown chequered bulk of a wren
looming behind him in the bush
and with a sudden start he was gone

Urchin

released by winter's storm
you lay on wave washed shingle
below the crumbled cliff
your five rayed symmetry
outlined in tiny pinpricks
the shape of a heart
long since solidified
and turned to stone

I imagined Mary who scoured
this tideline almost every day
her life dependent on your kind
on the waved frond of sea lily
the bullets of belemnites
bronze gleam of snakestone
the poke of devil's toe nail
even the fins of fish lizards

your cousins still burrow
in the sands of today
I found their fragile tests
tumbled clean by the waves
but still whole as far apart
as Ynyslas and Luskentyre
now you share the same shelf
lie together joined only by time

Birds in scarlet berries

The continent stripped bare,
hunger drove them to our shore.
Vikings irrupt on the east coast
in search of scarlet plunder.

Black masked bandits rape the rowan
gulp down whole one after another, another.
Pink soft silky plumage, tufted crests,
flight feathers dipped in sealing wax.

Waxwings on rowans,
glimmers of summer light
through dull grey days,
omens of glacial cold, a waxwing winter.

Terrorists

grey ones hawk about the country searching

she slips in plants the charge unseen

disguised to suit her special target hidden

a dozen time bombs to slavery ticking

the gentle shell kills by stealth breaking

a secret weapon in each home growing

all opposition put to flight routed

over the edge into oblivion falling

he only sits keeps watch calling

the twofold note from the hedges echoes

the infamous voice stops the bird has flown silence

left to make their own way home unknown

Famous Poems

*Words inspired by other more
famous poems with a twist
Apologies to all the original poets*

Stop   20
Port Selda   21
Lorries   22
Initially   23
Is the loo free   24
Stopping by floods   25
Shop fever   26

Stop

all the cars, close down all the banks that loan,
gag the politician's ceaseless drone.
Cleanse the traffic fumes, silence the intruding hum,
if the earth becomes a coffin, no mourners will come.

Let no airplanes circle, pollute the sky,
repair the hole in the ozone, we're not going to die.
Listen, do what the environmentalist asks,
let the policemen take off their respirator masks.

Let Summer, Autumn, Winter and sweet Spring
through tropical, temperate and arctic bring
the sunrise and the sunset every day,
let the world remain for our children to play.

See that the stars still shine in the Milky Way,
light up the moon, rekindle the sun's ray.
Keep the ocean full, grow once again the wood,
live for our future, it can only be good.

Port Selda

Yes, I remember Port Selda,
the name, because one morning
the boat moored there
unscheduled, due to the storm.
The waves crashed, the boat rocked,
no-one disembarked or boarded
on the windswept deck. What I saw
was Port Selda, from a distance,
and waves, waves and rocks,
and the sand and the rolling horizon.
Never still, never calm,
and clouds raging across the sky
and for a moment an albatross hung
above the mast and around him
gathered in great flocks, half the gulls
of the northern and southern hemispheres.

Lorries

Eddie is from Cumbria and Norbert from France
up and down the motorway they run to and fro
with a cargo of groceries
tins of beans and sausages
apples pears and plums and all things that grow.

Supply chain logistics that spreads far and wide
all around the country and the continent
with a cargo of essentials
that everybody needs
always delivered wherever they are sent.

Dirty old dustcart going to the tip
fighting through the traffic on a wet winter's day
with a cargo of rubbish
that nobody wants
bury in the earth let it rot away.

Initially

You're a bit of a duffer if you can't get CA.
PB is lead but you wouldn't call his heavy.
ST wasn't a saint and she wasn't either.
GM and EB are coloured earth and gravy.
Another GM is black as hauling over and
don't miss the next GM hovering around.
WC is unfortunate, could be, but isn't Welsh.
AC is nothing at all to do with electricity.
You'd be forgiven if you thought AJ was a girl.
For HC take shelter somewhere in fairy land.
RLB didn't shine a light of any kind and
by George it certainly isn't rocket science.
To finish something a little bit harder, FSCJG,
could be a short trainee killer whale in Latin.

You can even try it the other way round.
John Ronald Reuel rings a bell eagerly.
You know William Butler didn't wait at table.
Time didn't stop for long for Wystan Hugh.
Whilst Thomas Stearns has only got one L.
To track David Herbert home just follow Clint
but Thomas Edward on the hill clouds the view.
Alfred Edward was a county lad who liked cherries.
Ronald Stuart worshipped both god and tractor.
Frederick William just loved his home county.
Edward Estlin is the opposite of going repeatedly.
Patrick Joseph's, Beatles played there less R but with it.
And, if you really want to scratch your head,
Eric Barry Wilfrid sounds like a bloke's greeting.

Is the loo free?

I will arise and go now
and go for a little pee
in the small room built there
of plastic and porcelain made
nine loo rolls shall I have there
and a brush for the lavatory
and sit alone on the china throne.

and I will sit quietly there
whilst peace comes over me
dropping from the cobwebs on the ceiling
to where the loo brush stands below
whether it's in the glimmer of morning
or under noon's hot shining sun
or in the evening full of the bat's wing.

I must arise and wait now
because I really need to go
I hear loo water lapping
with low sounds through the door
whilst I stand cross legged in the hallway
waiting for the water to fall
I hear it, I hear it, in the bladder's deep call.

Stopping by floods on a rainy evening

Whose fields are these I'm not quite sure
but the rivers rising higher
and they won't see me drive through here
through their green fields flooded over

My 4x4 will get across
who needs a hard road to follow
rain has flooded these lush meadows
between wood and swollen river

Other than the revving engine
the only sound the liquid splash
of water underneath the wheels
then lapping right up to the doors

The fields are flooded dark and deep
and water has begun to seep
with miles to go before I reach
with miles to go before I reach

Shop fever

I must go down to the shops again
to the crowded superstore throng
and all I ask is an empty aisle
and a trolley to push along
with a wobbly wheel with squeaking song
and all those offers waiting
and the sad look on the checkout's face
and the false smile breaking

I must go down to the shops again
for the groaning shelves are calling
They're stacked so tall they're bound to fall
the health and safety's appalling
and all I ask is a two for one
or a buy one get one free
and the extra points just for me
that's how your shopping should be

I must go down to the shops again
for the umpteenth time today
to the endless bargains special deals
how on earth can I keep away
and all I ask is a quick exit
when I reach the end of the queue
and a bag with a decent bottom
that my shopping doesn't drop through

Worcester and Cathedral

From the many workshops attended in the Cathedral and around the City

Billycock	*28*
Diglis	*29*
Drover	*30*
Halloween 14	*31*
The herb garden	*32*
Here	*33*
Locked	*34*
Peal of flowers	*35*
All these	*36*

Billycock

Billy's me name
bow aulin's the game
you can tell me trade
by me billycock at
and me muscular build
wadin for miles through water
or tramping through farmer's crops
haulin on me rope
attached to the mast
wearin me ash bough frame
wiv me leather arness
takes up to eighty of us
to aul three undred tons
seventy feet of trow
wide in the beam
low in the water
always answers
too slow to the tiller
takin the milk to Bournville
every day every bleedin day

Diglis

I was born on the banks of Sabrina's river
my bed still lies beside her stream
beside the tow path bright with flowers
purple loosestrife spikes yellow tansy buttons
the pungent whiff of horseradish
my roads were dock navigation basin trow way
bouncing on the swinging bridge as water foams beneath

I grew to love the noisy swirl of rising fish
that fleeting flash of silver
the swans serene whose black tipped orange beaks
with black diamond cheeks that point to darker eye
nibbling green streamers from the basin wall
then heads laid back on sinuous necks
preening pure whiteness of folded wing

I grew to love that metallic handle clank
and the mesh of gears
the water's well and spurt
the creak of heavy gate
the strain it took to move five tons
the slow opening the prow emerging
a shadow from the night

I grew to love those water roads
only one lock to Tewkesbury sixteen miles
only thirteen to Stourport three locks this time
or twenty nine miles to Gloucester three locks again
and if you were brave enough to take the road
to Birmingham just thirty miles
but fifty eight locks to slow your way

Drover

Come down from the mountains.
Follow the old tracks to Worcester.
Wait for the tide to turn
to avoid the flood,
the stink from the tan pits
and skin yard sharp in
our dusty nostrils.

Down through the Bullring,
count through the Cripplegate,
pay the toll over the bridge
and on to the market.

After the sale, the Bush,
the Bear, the Cock, to
quench our parched throats,
before a welcome bed for the night.

Tomorrow, the long road home.

Halloween 14

A monumental memorial, a shell crater,
sheets of steel embedded in earth.
The panels reach higher as the bodies pile,
rusted rulers measuring the dead.

From above a huge flower, a shattered bloom,
metal petals split and spread.
All those lives blown apart,
laid to rest, commemorate the dead.

It was autumn then, but spring now.
Today, daffodil leaves become bayonets,
a coil of fern unfolds the regimental flag
pulmonaria leaves froth flecked from gas blown lungs.

From 'Plug Street Wood' to the chateau,
the names, the medals, recall those lost.
Major Hankey, Brace, Evans, Powell, Swift,
Worcester men all and many more.

Death was not as clear cut as this.
Death was dirty, messy, blood not rust.
May we always give thanks and remember
as we lay the ghosts of Gheluvelt to rest.

The herb garden

A thousand fingers point the way.
Steer the chariots drawn by doves
twixt devil's and dunny nettles.
Follow the trail the blue sailors sail.

Find Jack behind the garden gate,
the herb of grace, the green ginger,
Mary's milk-drops, the freckled face.
Beware marsh malice and snake's pie.

Listen to the church bells chime to
welcome the queen of the meadow.
Lad's love beds ladies in the hay,
fairy fingers pick their lockets.

Watch golden drops of evening fall
as long legs dampen in the dew.
The flicker of moth's moonflower
lit by the glow of evening star.

Here

Come, make pilgrimage to this green hill.
Come, gaze in wonder at your city.

Here, where your own cannon were turned
on your cathedral, levelled your city walls.

Here, where English justice was fought for,
where King John still stirs in his tomb.

Here, where men of renown made pilgrimage
from far across the western ocean wide.

Here, where they stood in reverence,
on this hill, where democracy was born.

Here, where they could not understand
how we forgot where liberty was fought for.

Loud rings the bell from that far shore,
proclaiming liberty throughout the land.

Tall stands the statue, freedom's icon,
enlightening the world.

Here, where the grant of liberty was fought for,
the gift to live in freedom first given.

Locked

the handle engages cogs clank and turn
lift the sluice the gush and boil of water
the muddied smell flotsam bobs and bounces away
with the flow to the waiting mallard and moorhen

lean heavily strain to start against the unseen current
the gate creaks slowly open onto a new stretch
slip slowly from between the steep dripping walls
out into the stream and softness of light again

the thrum of the engine's echo lingers
with the fumes in the enclosed air
the rainbow slick coating the levelled surface
of the vacuum left by the boat's departure
the space to be filled by the next traveller
floating on a cube of water down the canal

above in the light there is knapweed and thistle
mingled with the starry white umbels of angelica
butterflies seek nectar roam from head to head
bright new tortoiseshells not so common blues
the breeze ruffles the sweet-grass edging the cut
the hedge brown at home in this corridor of peace
patrols up and down keeping the gates of the lock

A peal of flowers

a wash of bells peals through
the sunlit blue of anemones
ringing welcome to the light
shining bright on yellow celandines
from their leaves green glossiness
the first real breath of spring breathes
amongst the nodding daffodils
the air is filled with notes of bells
and see the bees visit for sweet nectar
flit from head to head dipping deep
the honey the bumble and furry bee fly
now yellow then blue and blue blue
amongst this sea of flowers
here and there a pure head of white
whilst all around the sounds spread
the flowers tremble slightly in the sun
is it the wind or the bells vibrations
that reach down into the ground
the bells that continuously sound
round and around round and around

All these

all these ought to be spoken
all these ought to be heard
all these could make a poem
from the sound of the spoken word

I heard the sleek hulls slicing the surface
the rumble of seats slide along the boat
the oars skittering over the water
the repeated rhythm of the stroke
the cathedral bell strike eleven

I heard twin kayaks cutting the water
their stereo paddle strokes
the waspish buzz of an outboard
the slop of wash against the shore
the falling of a leaf to earth

I heard paired footsteps along the towpath
one heavy plodding and slow
the other tripping light and fast
the harsh caw of a crow
children scuffing through the leaves

I heard the trundle of a pushchair
the tick tick of a bicycle wheel
the slap slap of swans wings on water
the sigh of wind through the trees
the cathedral bell strike twelve

all these have been spoken
all these have been heard
all these have made a poem
from the power of the spoken word

all these

Evesham and the Vale

*I grew up in the Vale market gardens
picking all the vegetables and fruit.
In those days you could still hear
the local dialect 'Asum grammar.'*

SummutupinAsum	38
Pick of the crop	39
Canapés	40
The Vale	42
Where is this place	43
A few instructions	44
I am a town	45
Caribbean	46

SummutupinAsum

Thur bist summutup wivit yew,
thow knowdst, thur way we seztak.
Sosez newuns rownyur anyroad,
them that spakes wiv plums in thur mouves.
Bist offen our trees, Oill bet thu.
What dusthay think theym doin
poncin abart like thaydust
thaydunt know bugger all yew.

Wishumud keep thur noses out
lerrus gerron wivourown wuk.
Meantusay yew tak growin tak
theyudnt a bluddy clew yew.
Cudnt tell a byun from a pay.
Thay udnt even know a clat
if theyd triptoverun woodum.
Drive a tractur, thatud be alarf.

Thay couldnst plough strait if thay tryed,
it taks a bit a nohow yew.
Jusamaginum hooin now,
scrat the bleedin lotup woodennum.
What abart sprartpickin then,
iffenit wur frosty as like.
Theedst never get the buggers owtabed wudthe,
not when um cracks off the stoms yew.

Think theyd beeyunnygood with a shuppick
Ittud dootu stickumup tharse wiv,
thatud wakum uppabit wouldnst.
I guttaell yew theym makin me wild.
Summutup, oill give thee summutup,
Thay canst mind thur own bluddy bisniss yew.

Pick of the crop

I only ever had one claim to fame
picking plums was the name of the game
I tried Czars and Eggs purple and yellow
Prolifics Damsons too little too slow
plump Victorias were by far the best
you couldn't afford to stop for a rest
each box to fill was half a hundred weight
you had to pick at one hell of a rate
you dare not slow down and you dare not stop
you just picked and picked till they reached the top
seven till five with a break for dinner
you just kept right on to be the winner
you went on and on until you were done
box after box till you reached the ton
clamber up and down ladders rung by rung
pick all those fruit clusters from where they hung
push among twigs and leaves for all those plums
fill one more box before the tractor comes
now just look at your hands they're not very nice
broken nails cut fingers you paid the price
aching arms aching legs aching back
then all the skin on your hands starts to crack
it was piecework each box was half a crown
no leaves or twigs or stones to weigh it down
that was five pounds a day seven days a week
pick on and on as your fortune you seek
now you're done and dusted feel at a loss
award yourself the Victoria Cross

Canapés

Dust thee remembur when we wuz at that posh do.
I reckon it wur in the Public all, when it wuz still open yew.
Cant remembur fur the luv a me what it wuz in aid of.
Tu celebrate summut important yew, musta bin.
Best bib and tucker yew, dubbined me ob nails up didn I.
Fresh baler twine fur me trowsers.
Saves me belt fur the plum pickin dunt it.

Thay giv us them fancy glasses
with a splash a that fizzy tack in the bottom,
one swaller and it were gone, wunnit.
Then sum poncey git cum over and he sez, posh like,

Would you like some canapés sir?

Well I thort it a bit strange yew, but well, corse I ud,
yew ud, wudnt yew. Well, I thought Smedleys didn I,
nice tin a best garden pays, guz down well yunytime, dunnit.
You knowz, it were bout the time a that
fresh as the moment when the pod went bluddy pop bloke.
Thort it a bit strange yew, next thing I urd he wuz opnin wun o
them fancy new sportz shops up thu Igh street.

Dust yew remembur aving tu fill up them nets with twenny punds
a the little buggers. Ard work that wuz,
bluddy pay hom, tangles round yer legs summut chronic.

Anyroad, I wusnt gooin to turn down a can a pays was I,
so I sez yes, dunt I. That wuz a mistake werent it.

Quick as a flash e stuck this plate o stuff right under me nose.

Well, I gutta ell an back yew, talk bout small,
they wuz bluddy minute yew, wudnt av fed a field mouse,
letlone wun a them rats yew gets round yer barn.

Go on sir, try one, they are very tasty, e sez, so I does, dunt I.

Ardly got a taste of summut and then it was gorn yew.
Went to get another but eed shot orf cross the room,
giv um all away.

An that wuz afor I cud ask im
where thee ell me can uv Smedleys wuz, too.

Followd im round fur a bit
but e kept lookin over is shoulder at me,
an then e scarpered, never did see im aguyn did I,
what abart yew? Bit of a rum do if you arsk me.
What was it yew, dunst thee remembur?

Musta bin one a them Dewbillees or summut like that.

Never did get me bluddy can a pays did I.

The Vale

tufts of old mans beard wave
silver in sunlight against blue sky
tall spears of mullein sway
shower seed along the verge
secret beneath the soil lie
the balled roots of orchids
sunlight stored ready
to send up spotted leaves
and pink pyramids next year
a kestrel glides on thermals
banks and slips along the ridge
hangs on quivering wingtips
then drops like a stone
buzzards ride the up-draught
flight paths criss and cross
as they circle up and up
the swollen river tumbles over
the weir into a froth of
swirling brown foam
rushes away downstream
across the plain the humped
whale of Bredon rises
crowned by tree and tower
gazes down across the Vale

Where is this place

where I was born, from which I have grown,
this green garden upon a green hill,
where the river winds around the town
and meanders gently across the Vale.

This market place, this midland shire,
to which I am rooted, in which I reside,
where the ghosts of 'Eof' and 'De Montfort'
still haunt the market gardener's fields.

Where asparagus spears the springtime
and the stick beans run up the poles,
the summer juice of plums dribbles,
and frozen sprouts cling to the stem.

The soft contours of the valley
take shelter under Bredon's dome,
In the breeze the Vale blossom snows,
the trees hang heavy with fruit.

Where Cotswold beeches sigh on the ridge,
cropped grass bleaches over Malvern rock,
the Avon meadows silver with flood.
It is here, Evesham, and I am home.

**A few instructions on the art of
plum picking in the Vale of Evesham**

Weema sturtin upput top piece turday lads
Gotter cart thu laddurs an tak up thur fust
Twennnyuns ulldo thjob thay byunt too tall
That thur bloody frost in May gotatum yew
Bist only a fur crop but theym a gud size
Dunst thee furget theest pickinover wilst thu
No greenuns or rottununs now utherwise
theymll goo bad afur thay gets tur markut
Fillemup well now soasm bangs thu scales down
An makeshur yew keeps them thur leaves an stoms owt
Mindun stackum soas tractur can getattum
Iffit sturts wettin coverumup kwiklike
Thee pudst unnywetuns in yew thayll sweatup.

Ow much yer thinkin of payin owt then boss

Iffun yew picksum well ill give yu shillin a chip
But only if thaym gooduns cant say fairurn that
Best price inthairea yew wunt gettno bettur
Well whatheehell yew standin arounyer fur
getton wivvit yew lot weyunt got aullday
Wants a loadoff afore breakfust fur turdays markut

I am a town

I'm a town among the shires, I've a road that goes right through.
You can call in for a coffee if you want to brave the queue.
I'm cheap petrol should you need it, if you're travelling very far.
I am cigarettes and chewing gum, I am fumes you leave behind.

I'm asparagus in the springtime and plums from a roadside stall.
I'm the grammar of the locals, a dialect with a drawl.
I'm the churches on the skyline, and the tall Bell Tower too.
The Abbey soaring above them, King Henry laid to ruin.

My orchards hang with fruit, a market gardener's eden.
Their dreams are filled with plenty if only they could reach them.

I am a town.

I am All Saints just for the townsfolk, from local Blue Lias clay.
I'm Saint Lawrence for the pilgrims, to keep the plague away.
I remember in the quietness, alone in my old age.
I'm not sure where you're going, I hang on to my old ways.

I am a town.

I'm a town lying in the Vale, I am pickers in the fields.
I'm an old tractor in the yard, weeds between my wheels.
I'm Asum Gold ale, England's garden,
in Worcester's fair shire found

I am there behind the bypass sign, as you drive straight round.

I am a town. I am a town. I am a town.

Evesham found.

Caribbean

well I gu tu ell an back yew
that thur spellin unt up tu much
strange that thay shud want poems
about how to carry byuns
carry byuns by ek we did
used ter lug em all down the rows
tween them thur sticks up which they growd
chips of em hangin on yer arms till they was dyud
cut yer fingers till they all but bled
If it wur wet they bist a evy load
four at a time wus all yew cud old
remember what the boss man said
be sure theest picks strait uns yew
no old or curly uns
just the longest and greenest that grew
off theyd cum fresh as cud be
the Vales finest for all to see
carry em up to the end of the piece
where the lorry stands weigh each chip
add the cover and rubber bands
down the road to Asum markut
till the price crashes cos of the glut
then rotovate the buggers into the ground
and wait to carry byuns next summer round

Croome

*From many hours spent as a volunteer
for the National Trust at Croome
when the park first opened*

After the storm	48
Ballet	49
Drought	50
The Owl's seat	51
Reverie	52
Sea of green	53
Singing leaves	54

After the storm

comes the intensity of stillness
the smell of damp earth rises
confetti petals litter the path
dripping trees flit with birds
swallows skim the meadows
weave through grass stems
the dandelion clocks are bare
time blown away
the scent of lilac and laburnum
bluebell and broom
and may
all mixed together
fresh green leaf boats drift
on the muddied waters
a collage of reed stems
blown into the lake corner
the still dark sky is lit
by a thousand candles
aflame on the horse chestnuts

Ballet

white frost fingers grass and leaf
blue sky jet streams reflect in the lake
flies cluster like a salvo of bullet holes
bask on the warm patterned bark of a plane
a bead of water drops from an orange beak
slides off a coot's back as it bobs to the surface
head on from the bridge the neck of the cob
slices the heart of white arched wings
the skater sliding smoothly over glass
swans in tandem like some strange serpent
dance patterns in the water call to each other
a head turns gazes then plunges below to feed
circles of light leap from ripple to ripple
spreading…….. spreading…….

Drought

A buzzard rides the already rising thermals,
beneath, the meadow hums with grasshoppers.
The tractor cutting the hay wends it way
around the field in ever decreasing circles.
From the ridge crows form dot to dot
patterns on the freshly shorn grass.
The sharp scent of broom lifts on the still air,
lavender swarms with meadow browns.
Clouds build as the thunder
mutters through the horizon haze,
rumbles around a pregnant sky.
Stones and mud banks show at the lake's edge,
the water several feet lower than normal.
Skullcap, gipsywort, forget-me-not
and water plantain have colonised
around the exposed brown band.
A second brood of mallard chicks forage,
shepherded by a patient mother.
The reflections fade as the
freshening breeze obscures the mirror.
Surely it will, it must, rain soon.

The Owl's seat

the pellets proclaim ownership
or at least squatters rights
to the view across the plain
along the sweeping curve of river
toward the stately court
the heron patrols the margins
with white wing barred
piping waders and wagtails
whilst the cob swan chases
the intruding canadas
through a raft of tufted ducks
that dive and bob between
a woodpecker laughs then drums
from the stag headed oak
where the buzzard watches
in the short grass the leafy promise
of early purple orchids
braves the still frosty morning
yet the chiffchaff is here
sawing away and the nuthatch
hunts the trunks and flutes overhead
when the light dies and the night
and the owls come what happens then

Reverie

On the hill the door opens and closes,
sun flashes a morning signal
through the window of the church.
It lights the racing pigeon's wings
as they whistle low across
the meadow, startle the sheep.
On the grass a ring of feathers
from a sparrow hawk's kill
spreads slowly in the wind.
Flycatchers dance over the waters
of a lake muddy with sediment.
Reflected ripples of light from
the leaf debris patterning the water
coils and twists in the breeze.
Basking fry scatter at a shadow,
darter and hawker patrol the margins
above skullcap and gipsywort.
Long tailed tits seep and slip through
the green light of chestnut leaves.
In the middle of the field
a siege of herons holds sway.

Sea of green

out on the sea of green
the smooth surface ruffles
as wave after wave passes
now illuminated by the sun
then cloud darkened from above
all the heads are neatly aligned
then pushed and spread by the wind
they twist and turn sway and surge
then rise again as each wave passes
wait for the next and the next
then as the seed slowly ripens
each head grows slightly heavier
resists the wind that fraction more
as the sea of green grows taller

Singing leaves

they come
air darkens
clouds swirl and swoop
circle and alight
re-leaf treetops
with leaves that sing
that shuffle and shift
in non-existent breeze
sun sparkled breasts
glint in pale light
the whisper of a thousand tongues
beaks agape with gossip
spreads the news
clouds erupt as they leave
dissolve into silence
till only bare twigs remain
pointing to a cloudless sky

Inspirations

Experiences as you go through life that touch a chord and prompt a poetic response

Door	56
Each and every	57
Echoes	58
Peregrinatio pro amore Dei	59
Priest	60
The Saint's way	61
Song stream	62
Tide	63
T is for Tesco	64
Underneath	65

Door

I am a low door with an old latch
set in thick walls of time.
My lintel catches your head solidly,
ingrains a memory. All bow
as they pass through me, except
the child, who cannot reach my latch.

Many have passed over the years
since I was first hewn from the wood.
My jamb supports the space my boards fill.
Once closely lain above my head, they
carry old footprints, now walking walls.
Beaten hinges creak with age, squeal for oil.

I open to a new life as it enters or leaves,
or close to an old one on its final journey.
They pass both ways feeling my age.
Fingers rattle my latch, wear the paint away,
smooth my very heartwood down,
hand engraved by passing.

Each and every

Barely light, yet the kestrel already hangs
in front of a shepherd's warning.
Traffic piles on the motorway.
Crooked V's of gulls head for the tip
to a garbage breakfast.
Short back and sides hedges.
Rolls of straw sulk in the sodden fields.
Deer glean pale regrowth from the stubble.

Cotswold clarity after rain,
the details pull you in, spire, tower.
Dazzling below the visor the sun
strikes white under a pigeon's wing,
heightens the sheen of a crow's back,
traces ridge and furrow fingers up the slope.
Windows flash from the ribbon
that glistens up the hill.

Clouds build behind the ridge then overspill,
pouring vapour downslope that wreathes and vanishes.
Bows of coloured light show between each stroke
before the screen opaques again.
The banded horizon fades through cream, to steel,
to midnight blue. Bitter prophecy of frost
as the cold sucks the light from the sky.

Echoes

Words assigned, placed for all time,
by people that dwelt on the land.
Generations pass, slowly bed in.
Successive mouths wear syllables
as water and wind wear rock.
Rounded, slipped from tongue to tongue,
lost meanings sunk deep in earth.
Names that outlast language
rise from submerged races
the talk of forgotten tribes.
Strands woven in culture,
the warp threads of history,
still there for us all to hear.

Peregrinatio pro amore Dei

beyond the edge of the world
adrift on a desolate grey sea
at the mercy of wind and tide
in search of peace

all that kept them afloat the
tension in curved hazel rods
that strained taut the fat smeared hides
the holly resin that sealed the joints

would their salt stung eyes
ever see the smudge of land
break the blank horizon's heave
their feet ever touch earth again

Fionán to Skellig
Columcille to Iona
Brendan all the way to America
all they took was faith

Priest

They rise and splash in the holding pool,
flash as they leap the waterfall,
that glint of liquid mercury scale,
in peat stream, under moonlight pale.

Caught in the net as it closes round,
hush my silver beauties, splash no more,
for sound travels far over water
in the stillness of the night.

No more to strain, to pull the line tight,
never give up without a fight.
Time to put you quietly to sleep,
let the priest administer the last rite.

Heavy in hand, they deal out death.
A tap on the head, leather and lead.
Stun the fish, take a final breath,
shush, was that a salmon or a bailiff?

The Saint's way

rest weary legs on sun warmed rocks
wait for the tide to turn
as it does so the waders appear
flicker in twists and turns
to alight at the water's edge
follow the sea as it ebbs

this the last leg to Lindisfarne
all the way from Melrose
stride out onto the causeway
that uncovers before us
still lapped with salt water
at last we reach the holy isle

scrunch onto gravelly sand
search the sea for his ducks
scour the beach for fossil lilies
grown in the meadows of the sea
dismembered by countless tides
into the star stones of Cuthbert's beads

Song stream

I am the rain that drops from the cloud
the sleet that rattles the window pane
the hail that bounces from the ground
the snow that silently blankets all

I am the trickle that wells from the earth
the bubble that issues from the spring
the liquid that oozes from the peat
the seep from the solid rock

I am the tinkle of the tiny rill
the sunlit ripple of the brook
the chatter of the flowing beck
the white water tumble of the burn

I am the slow glide of the river
the wearing down of the valley
the meander through the meadow
the stillness of backwater calm

I am the creek that cuts through the marsh
the winding through shoal and sandbank
the broad sweep of the bleak estuary
the flow into the ever restless sea

Tide

saturated night steeped in dankness
the leaden sky oozes fluid from congealed dark
oil black it reclaims the land once more
the froth edged rime creeps shoreward
sponges bird track mazes from the fossil surface

moon tugged it leaks imperceptibly over the slime
swallows cold glint of mussel mother of pearl
floats empty mermaid's purses currency spent
consumes a jellyfish the festering mucous moon
gleams among the broken arms of brittle stars

licks over tiny crests of current rippled floor
pebbles chatter response the trickle turns to flood
laking unseen hollows in the shifting sands
hermits stir from shelled houses scavenge flotsam
barnacle oarsmen row water strain saline soup

the red eye stab of a crisp packet cuts the flatness
cellophane sail filled by a brine edged wind
it scuds over the shallows onto fucus netted rock
operculi unlatch bodies slime from shells
radula rasp graze the rock pool gardens

mining the worm riddled seams of mud
the spaded bait digger retreats trailing jagged castles
the shell shocked holes gape like giant footprints
then slowly moat leaving a chain of mirrors
reflecting silver from a fish scaled sky

T is for ......

Tea eggs sugar cheese oxo
Tiramisu evian sangria coffee oranges
Tomatoes elderflower sprouts cucumber onions
Target every single consumer opportunity
Television electrical saucepan computer odour-eaters
T shirt espadrilles socks cardigan overcoat
Turmeric enchiladas sauerkraut chillies oregano
Total eclipse small competition obliteration
Tissues envelopes sausages carrots oxtail
Tabasco emmenthal strudel calabrese oatcakes
Tequila extra points salt coconut olives
Till everyone shops complete obedience

Underneath

The missile fashioned fired from a bow
aimed by an eye that couldn't see
slew his brother

A mother's tears rained down on me
from whence the arrow came
banished from the fletcher's realm
here suspended I must remain

Cut me as the year turns
take care for if I touch
the earth the magic drains
hang as the clock strikes twelve
before you burn the old

Be wary of the speckled bird
yet need him so you can fly
wipe sticky beak upon the bough
push my sinker in slowly bleed the tree

The legend lingers on
make the barren fertile
counteract the drug
pluck translucent berry
beware the kiss below

About the Author

Born & bred & still living in the Vale of Evesham Bob Woodroofe's poems appear in many poetry magazines & are performed locally. Inspired by the natural world, the landscape & local tradition he attempts to bring the magic of nature & its restorative & healing qualities to a wider audience.

Also available from the

Greenwood Press

38 Birch Avenue, Evesham
Worcs. WR11 1YJ

website http://greenwoodpress.co.uk

e-mail info@greenwoodpress.co.uk

by Bob Woodroofe

A trilogy of poetry collections from
life & nature in the Vale of Evesham

Nature, Reflections & Spirit of the Vale

In search of greenness

Something Stirred

the Poetry Collection

Pick of the crop

Joint poetry collections by
Sue Johnson & Bob Woodroofe

Tales of Trees & Journey

Creative Writing books
by Sue Johnson

Writer's Toolkit & Writer's Toolkit 2, 3 & 4

www.ingramcontent.com/pod-product-compliance
Lightning Source LLC
Chambersburg PA
CBHW031459040426
42444CB00007B/1150